FINISHING LINE PRESS

www.finishinglinepress.com

TANGO MAN

poems by

Doreen Stock

Finishing Line Press
Georgetown, Kentucky

El Otro

De donde viene esa mirada
que veces sube hasta mis ojos
cuando los dejo sobre un rostro
descansar de tantas distancias?

Es como un agua en cisterna
que brota desde su misterio,
profundidad fuera del tiempo
donde el recuerdo oscuro tiembla.

Metamorfosis, doble rapto
que me descubre el ser distino
tras esa identidad que finjo
con el mirar enajenado.

Marcelo Holot

The Other

Where does that look come from
rising up into my eyes at times
when I allow them to rest on a face
at such distances?

It's like water in a cistern
bubbling up from its mystery,
from depth outside of time
where dark memory trembles.

Metamorphosis, double rapture
that I uncover beyond this identity
that I pretend to, a different self
with gaze transported.

*Translated from the Spanish of Julio Cortezar
by Doreen Stock*

TANGO MAN

for Marcelo
el otro, de verdad

ACKNOWLEDGMENTS

The author wishes to thank these publications in which the following poems
first appeared:

Tango Man, *Marin Poetry Center Anthology*, Volume XV, 2012,
New Song of Songs, published as a broadside by Benicia Historical Society
and Public Library for their annual Love Poetry Contest, 2012.
Vine in Leaf; We Were Speaking of Picasso, *California Quarterly*, Summer,
2019
Swimming the Black-Flagged Sea, *Marin Poetry Center Anthology*, Volume
XX, 2019.

Also thanks to Leah Maines for selecting this manuscript, to the entire staff
at Finishing Line Press, to Jack Hirschman for his words on it, and to all
writing buddies in North Beach, SF and Marin, with special gratitude to
Jaqueline Kudler, Kathy Evans, and Barbara Swift Brauer who received and
commented on these poems, to Laurel Feigenbaum who helped shape and
titled *Tango Man*, and to Cathy Shea for tech support.

Publisher: Leah Maines
Editor: Christen Kincaid
Cover Art: Amy Stock Drozd
Author Photo: Marcelo Holot
Cover Design: Elizabeth Maines McCleavy
Copy Editor: Judy Brackett Crowe

Order online: www.finishinglinepress.com
also available on amazon.com

Author inquiries and mail orders:
Finishing Line Press
P. O. Box 1626
Georgetown, Kentucky 40324
U. S. A.

Table of Contents

Tango Man

In my dream I was flying over Argentina, Love, looking down at its form, larger than politics or geography and darkly lit. I saw your country, Tango Man, laid out like one big steak on a cosmic *parilla*; the place where sailing from Minsk and Moldavia they met, your people, to fold you into history there, where the top brass polished their boots over you not far from the alleyway where Evita Duarte dreamed her big dreams, and the Plaza San Martín where Jorge Luis Borges could imagine the two of us as teenagers, and right there on his park bench pull out his old coin and give it to us instead of to his Other, so we would wake up and meet in the center of your dance palace, Tango Man.

"I'm an anarchist, but not the boom-boom kind," you said to disarm me. Little did I know it was the absolute truth: no bedtime, no waking-up time, no shaving time, absolutely no dressing time, no close-the-window time, at your wrist only *porteño* time, so we'll always know when the Rio de la Plata streams nickel under the moon and always pen-in-your-hand-into-love time as you concoct tango after tango, trying for the perfect embrace to fit me into our love song, the Argentine tango always written through tears. "We are sad here," said Piazzolla thoughtfully, as you are sad, so loving that dark, mean, sparkling land moving beneath me, and yet never enough to want to go home.

Sing, Tango Man, sing a song of no supper, no woman, no work, no currency, no government to keep you warm, bandits squatting in your house, and all the time the Plata moving between its shores, sluggish, dirty, with its terrible secrets, while black shoes, lit stage, violins and *bandoneons* wail at skirts slit, leg over leg entwining, *eso, eso*, slithering, lifting, drawing whole bodies into flight over your homeland, love, to which you never ever want to return.

How about we choose sunlight, a bright day to go back, a day when the Plata is blue and the buildings stand still in their whiteness and those big *palo borachos* in the square are heavy with *flores* and the dog walkers of Recoleta running on the grass under them with five, six pups on each hand, and the flea market wide open before the cemetery gates to all the old important graves, the dead chuckling, sighing, shattering in their stone houses. Burnt down to our bones we could fly there, on the eyelids of the river gulls, in time, before history wrote its horrible story inside you, when you were thirteen and she was crossing the dance floor in black pants, red shoes to invite you, remember her incredible skin so bright, her hair like a blackbird's feathers, and then you were flying, Tango Man, your very first tango, you could choose to go back into that...

Not Being Bombed

*"Under Trump, the United States has dropped about 20,650 bombs
through July 31, or 80 percent the number dropped under Obama
for the entirety of 2016."*

foreignpolicy.com

I breathe in not being bombed poach two eggs in boiling water
with a little white vinegar to make the whites perfect not being
bombed lift them from the water place them without breaking
the yolks on two slices of buttered whole-wheat toast without
being bombed place your breakfast before you unfold the news
paper not being bombed place fork and knife on each side of
your plate not being bombed bring a Lipton tea with milk
and sugar not being bombed kiss you not being bombed the part
under your moustache not being bombed straighten up not
being bombed sit opposite you at the table with a plate egg
toast fork knife napkin and green tea.

So far we have not been bombed, or if you have, you have not
told me yet or I have not found out yet from someone else, or
if I have, you have not been told by me or by a third
party. I watch you eat not being bombed eat it's good not being
bombed read an entire section of the newspaper not being bombed
while you do, too, and comment on one of the articles and launch
into a very long and involved History lesson courtesy of not being
bombed I manage to reach my own conclusions voiced or unvoiced
about what you have told me not being bombed I urge you Latin American
male that you are to carry your own plate to the sink not being bombed
you laugh and do it not being bombed I clear two cups, forks, knives, dirty
napkins do up the breakfast dishes including the poaching pan not being
bombed and not being bombed

I breathe out.

Eyeful of Horse, Lapful of Moon

After lunch we bed down. I lied
about the moonlight, actually it was
more like a quick tossed salad of hay
with brightness slanting in through the Venetian
blinds, a reunion of sorts, after which you snore
for two hours. I clean up the kitchen and ponder
some financial matters. Moonlight, no, but the horse
all sunny and blue did narrow his long eye in the space
just under the leather of his bridle.
It was dark as night in there.

Vine in Leaf

Your silken elbow bent just so one index finger
resting on the steering wheel while the other long
hand does its work to maneuver us at 75 mph
around the steaming big rig beside us blotting
out half an orchard but not those green canopies
hundreds of vines in leaf born new
this April and brightly respiring in California sun.
Can they hear us roaring past on Highway 5
busy as they are preparing their purples
training them at cellular level within their young
leaf-hood, silently schooling them cluster by cluster
in the ancient art of moving us a little closer to oblivion?

Full Moon on the Grand Canyon
July 7, 2009

"Mostly men fall in," said the ranger as we gathered at the
South Rim. "Statistically, it's the young ones," he added.
And as brightness bounced off of the cataracts beginning
to form in our aging eyes, your soft arm around me, your soft
hand in mine, what could we see, really, all the world's languages
murmuring through the crowd pressed at the edge of our cliff
hanging over the luminous greys?

"Attention!" whispered the French mom to the littlest one nodding
off at her side, none of the children under a certain age knowing why
their parents had dragged them out here, sensing, perhaps, something big,
the opposite of a mountain, "I'm hungry!" I heard one whisper, then, "Ahh!"
said one super-grown-up approaching the edge like a gourmet approaching
his favorite dish, but the children drowsed over the abyss imagining popcorn,
pizza and fudge as their elders stood trying to read designs of infinity through
the fishnet of wire.

Yes, we were all breathing, but suddenly before us waved a time of not
breathing at all, all done up in silver splendor, of course, but ominous as
are all things that beautiful, dreadful, really, as we walked on. And the only
light at the unreachable bottom gleamed up from a place called Phantom
Ranch where the super-rich dined on quail and wild rice flown down there
today just as the last Navajo was climbing up into the great white circle
above to tell of his people's sacrifice, a pack of coyotes lifting their voices
in echoing song.

We Were Speaking of Picasso

And your great left eye turned coal black
shoveling its way to the depths of mine,
this being miners' country (the local bar named
"The Diggin's")

And your great right eye turned silver (the color
you are trying to mix just this moment with a dab
of white, black, a breath of blue) and with the force

of a geological shift pushed the right half of your face
skyward with the peak of one of the Trinity Alps out-
lined in black trees along its spine and fog shrouded

the river flowing out of your sleeve creating
our past each second of this tree-shafted Friday

And the little squirrel you named *Maria* after a tango
scooted on the diagonal across the red deck flooring
for a morsel of Kellogg's Special K.

We Were Watching TV

And the pirate, *Sandokan*, Tiger of Malaysia, was off fighting
colonial powers on the South China Sea, while *Kukla*, a strange,
Groucho Marx-like character, and *Ollie*, the seasick sea serpent,
were bouncing around behind their cardboard stage the way hand
puppets do while their adult lady-friend, Fran, talked with them.

Sixty-six years ago. 4 p.m., local time, the six-year-old boy who was to
become you was sitting on a couch, a chair, or the floor in Buenos Aires
avidly watching the pirate, *Sandokan*. The eight-year-old-girl who was
to become me was watching the hand that was *Ollie*, the seasick sea
serpent, while sitting on a couch, a chair, or the floor in St. Paul,
Minnesota.

> It was all in black and white on small screens.
> We had yet to experience politics, love, war,
> birth, divorce, or death.

> We were watching TV.

Sun Setting Toward Argentina

You stayed in the rolled-up
car because of high, cold winds
and I walked out into
that last sunset
at Fort Cronkhite
not wanting to miss

the flaming sinking
knowing as the sand whipped
into my eyes and they teared
up and the beauty that sustains
us all, everything we eat,
everything we wear, beautiful
ball of gases burning, went down
into the curve of the earth heading
the whole 10,000 miles
toward Buenos Aires

where it will shine on you five hours
before it will shine on me, and where
it has already set, and where in a matter
of days your barber friend Rullo will cut
your hair and you will appear on my
computer screen shiny-faced, grinning,
all the beautiful hair that grew for months
on the pillow beside me, curling on the floor

that whatever you will grow down there
in rooms I've never seen and with people
I've never met, only the flaming sinking
knows, the little curls the sun grew here in
California into my kisses being swept up,
the cold sea pounding and emptying the slanted
shore between us, you so small behind glass, me
so solitary, this is the way we watched it, that last
flaming sinking away…

Cowboy in the Dark

Before the chain link-fence twisting its diamonds against
the backlit sky, little black end wires reaching up like
the news of torture from a prison, your face, the one I do love
beyond the grave, grins out at the person holding your camera
tonight, a full moon in Buenos Aires, and the fancy cowboy hat,
maybe it belongs to that person? There are no horses, no campfires
no pampas grass with herds of cattle stampeding through it
in the photo, only your Hollywood chin with the cleft in it jutting out
like it did that night at Mel's Dinner on Lombard Street where we ate
hamburgers after watching Salome slice John the Baptist's head
onto a plate, well, mine was a veggie burger. The moon here is so full,
Cowboy, the night so dreamy aching black.

And that's the beauty of a photo, Love. If there are stallions steaming
and running and a fire crackling to blazes where you are, at least
I can't see them.

We Missed another June

With that goofy smile that comes over you sometimes

another month of me staring at your moustache growing down toward your teeth and thinking it's time for you to trim it, and when you wrote about the full moon in Posadas, and how you saw it huge in that sky and thought of me, I was thinking of you, too.

I dreamt that you were monumental, like the Buddha himself, in your blue sweater and I jumped up there laughing into your blue eyes, which were slightly red from allergies courtesy of the dust in the little house in Misiones where you were staying and landed a kiss on your faraway

(a continent away, actually two continents because you have to fly to the East Coast first from here and then all the way down to Argentina)

mouth.

Paris, Gare Du Nord, Christmas Eve, 2008
December 25, 2005

In the bowels of the metro, fourth line, the purple one, just near the Rue Dunkerque station, three friends are celebrating the night that Christ was born.

The tall one without shoes, his feet cracked and grey, head resplendent in dreadlocks, tips the bottle of wine back toward his waiting gullet, a place I can only imagine, rumbling like the great chains of people whizzing past here, the little bells ringing, the doors slamming shut sounding each time like a puff of steam...

Friend number two in navy sweats and three thin jackets worn one over the other is bent over the third who lies stretched out on a bench, his bleeding face being wiped with a wad of cotton whiter than Santa's beard, glaringly white, chemical white, clenched in the shadowy hand of the other, making me wonder where on earth it came from, my eyes swiftly taking in the bound and bandaged feet of the wounded one receiving this gift of tenderness under the wall of little tiles that stretches upward from his midnight bed, his labored breath presided over by their blank surfaces...

We've just come from the Tower at Montparnasse where we danced a solitary tango on the rooftop and watched the great Boulevards below reflect their emptiness in scribbles of neon as the Eiffel Tower gave forth its hourly display of dazzling stars moving up and down its legs, like something out of Jacob's dream. And from taking a cold promenade on the Champs-Élysées lined with blue trees dripping electrical dew, the sound of cars rolling past us as we trudged toward the huge snowflake of a Ferris wheel parked at Place de la Concorde. The concierge at the Hotel Crillíon found for us the only restaurant left open in that neighborhood. And all the while we were eating (you, an Argentine, your steak, me, an aging hippy, my vegetables, washed down with a small champagne) these friends were arranging themselves to appear, a final tableau of farewell, as we exited this cave of a cathedral appearing as a train station, the woman from Bosnia with her signs in six languages, the Algerian with her two babies bundled into one stroller. And we left, for the last time, this palace of separation where the Grandes Lignes roll in and out on their tracks and the baguettes are stacked behind glass full of tomorrow's tomato, egg, and cheese, just beyond reach of so many mouths, moving past them, dying to eat them.

The Cigar of Fidel

For an instant
the horse poised
on the hill
happiness being the horse
human rights being the hill.
Fidel Castro has come to Chile
for the inauguration of Salvador Allende

and Fidel is smiling,
in his breast pocket
three Cuban cigars.

The Argentines, well-loved
because they have produced
Che, are given prime seats
at the inauguration of Allende
and an interview with Fidel.

You know how men clap each other
on the shoulder?

I am picturing Fidel clapping Marcelo
on his shoulder after he has asked: "Are these
the famous Cuban cigars made especially
for you?"
Fidel smiles.
Happiness *is* on the hill for an instant
and Fidel takes a cigar from his breast
pocket and gives it to Marcelo.
Of such small incidents History
is composed. Marcelo, although he doesn't
smoke, taking the cigar
thanking Fidel.

Let's say universal healthcare
is a human right
and is rolled up
in the brown paper.
Marcelo, when he returns to Argentina,
wraps the cigar and secretes it
in the depths of an attaché case.

Allende is assassinated.
The elegant horse
falling, falling from its moment
on the crest of the greenest hill.

What happens to this small souvenir of brief
happiness? It lies in the dark in an attaché case.
Marcelo doesn't smoke and not being in a position
of power in his own country he does not pass on
the cigar with a clap on the shoulder to someone else.
The crime rate continues to climb in Argentina.
Then on Marcelo's 64th birthday, which he is spending
at the Fairmont Hotel in San Francisco, a message from
a neighbor: his apartment has been *ocupado* by a gang
of thugs. He flies home, calls the police, and clears
the apartment, now cleaned out of all valuables, photograph
files, memorabilia, his dead wife's clothes. What did
the *ocupas* do with the souvenir of the moment of
happiness from the pocket of Fidel Castro? Pawing through
the attaché case and being apolitical as thugs are wont to be
(Wait. Hold that thought. We will examine it in its entirety
and all of its ramifications when we look back at our own
last election.)

Was the Havana cigar of Fidel tossed into the garbage?
Or did one *ocupa* unroll the paper, take the
now-stale moment of happiness wrapped around
universal healthcare and labeled with two white bands,
the first saying COHIBA, the second saying FIDEL CASTRO
in black, easy to read, and roll it between his thumb and two
fingers maybe holding it up to his fellow-thugs and say, "Anyone
want a puff of a stale Cuban cigar?" Then maybe they laughed
the *ocupa* laugh, not having an inkling, a clue, as to what
this is all about.

Swimming the Black-flagged Sea

When there are dangerous riptides
the life guards of Tel Aviv
raise small black flags
along this shore

Black flags and the incessant clack
of paddle tennis balls as the sun
broils down over the orange
umbrellas of Bograshov Beach

Black flags as the waiters in cool
glass-sealed reception rooms serve
little cups of mango sorbet to the guests
who have just flown in to inhabit the tall
hotels above

Black flags as the peddlers of Dreamsicles
shout out their wares in a tongue invented
from biblical phrases, pull them barely
melting out of blue styrofoam coolers
slung around their blistered necks hand
them out sweet and cold to naked toddlers
charging with little bare feet into the carefully
guarded yellow sand.

Black flags as you, red-rimmed
blue eyes flashing under a beige
hat today, here tell the tale
of Adolf Eichmann "And finish,"—you
ended, flattening out both hands like
an ump at home plate signaling the runner
safe.

I float in this warm turquoise sea
between the crashing waves
where Eichmann's ashes were
tossed, black salt into an open wound
eternally moving landward,
crystals breaking at this black-flagged border
we call the shore.

Should I never see you again, Love,
I would remember that you chose this
beach to tell me the tale of Adolf Eichmann
and that I was the one who swam
the black-flagged sea
with you waiting for me there
on what we call the shore.

A New Song of Songs

The lovers are now old.

The distance has been increased, one
lives in California, the other in Argentina.

Instead of calling out to one another in joyous song
they are reduced to texting in the green, green beginning
of the new spring, she imagining his blue eyes, his
long legs wrapped around her, he reciprocating by sending:

"The Jewish Agency invited me to a dinner. Now I am
writing from the place of the dinner, a house for old people.
I love you. I miss you. The dinner, chicken and peaches.
But nothing like to eat with you, my love."

This letter is endearing. But when she telephones he creates in her
such fury she vows to end the relationship. How will she
do it? A new *Song of Songs* is needed, one celebrating
the hills themselves, the sea itself, and not as a part of his body.
She struggles with this, pen in hand, for some time. It will not come
to her. To King Solomon, yes, every bit of the landscape has always
come to him, built palaces, bowers for him, has always sung for him,
but it does not for her.

And then Osama bin Laden is buried at sea. A new *Song of Songs*
filled with vengeance and grief is about to be written. She wants no
part of it.

What Happens in Geneva

She moves toward us dressed in red
dark hair gleaming like hair
heels clicking the polished surface
of the Woodrow Wilson Hotel banquet floor.

She, who has just been awarded the annual
UN Watch Human Rights Award for courage
and here confides the proudest moment in her life:
standing before the UN assembly to read
a section of her book into the faces of the Iranian
delegation: like a young slim Dostoevsky, her forehead
marked for execution, whip-lashed body bound to the posts,
hearing her schoolmate next to her fall, and being
suddenly swept into a black limo, saved by her interrogator
who, enamored of her, forced her to convert
to Islam and marry him while still serving her life
sentence in Evin, Tehran's infamous prison.

We clasp hands. I praise her work.
Time for just one question, "Weren't
you afraid of retribution?" I ask, naively.
She lets fly her signature Marina Nemat laugh.
"What could they do to me *now*? My book is
out! My story is told!"

Beyond us in the night, the long singular fountain
of this place sprays continually into the dark lake.
*"How many innocent lives are ending...?"** as
Marcelo's lips brush her ear. "We never cry about it
do we?" "Never!" she answers as they exchange
the long look of brother and sister.

*from *Requiem*, Anna Akhmatova

Kiss at the United Nations
Paris, June, 2011

In the seventh-floor lunch room of the UNESCO complex,
Place de Fontenoy, Métro Ségur, the Eiffel Tower up close
through the window, at my back the entire earth wrought
in metal spinning in formal gardens below.
You ate your Salmon Plate,
I ate my Vegetarian Composition.
You jumped up to meet someone in an office below and leaning
over the table pressed your lips to mine. The Kiss at the United Nations!
It fluttered on white wings so fast, up from that garden below, perhaps,
within this tall, orderly building with guards and meetings, lectures
and slideshows, papers and documents. You disappeared for a very long time.
I began to hear the babies crying in hellish places, a feeling the pristine
blue-and-white flag of this place cannot begin to convey...

Here one cannot see: the dove feathers blowing in hot wind,
feet bent around a black wire as if it were a bomb about to go
off, or the dead children littering the dusty roadsides.
Here one cannot hear: the scream of the bullet from the gun of an
eight-year-old soldier accomplishing his first kill.
Here one cannot feel the anguished sleep of the utterly betrayed.

We Tango at the Edge of the Sacred Valley
for Marcelo in his 70th Year
Machu Picchu, 2012

We met late
but not too late
We flew far
but not too far

We tango at the edge
of the Sacred Valley
You in your blue shirtsleeves
and squashed tourist hat
Me in my backpack
and, up there, after all those
stone steps, fresh dark lipstick?

A little short of breath
A little afraid of falling
A little unworthy, perhaps, to
behold all that has spread itself
beneath us. It could make us
dizzy, all those grey chambers
pushed skyward a giant honeycomb.
It could make us tremble,
all the heights vine-covered plushy
green, all the depths chartreuse grass
tucking itself in among the ruins.

Dizzy, trembling, hand in hand
you step forward, I step back.

If we fall, we fall.

Homage to Machu Picchu

I don't know the condor with his eye
that blinks from this world to the next,
his round white neck that awaits our final
transformation on his great wings, my love,
moving upward in this dark stone

I don't know the guinea pigs that swarmed toward this place
through little tunnels toward their final fire, the one stone altar
an image of their kind graced with an eye that gleams once a year
with the winter solstice sun

Nor do I know the lovely moon virgins, taught to weave and to cook
in their solitary school here that the chosen among them cross in white
leggings through the sacred rain into the great Inka's bedchamber,
more than one of them, it is said, for each night of the year, that the sun
god's chosen one open their wombs with his silver cornstalk of seed

Nor the young pure black llamas who steadfastly made their way
up and down the steep sides of this earth, grazing, nestling into these
grassy terraces until the day of their beheading, their hearts torn out of
their chests, heaving, offered up to the Sun

Nor the holy green domes of the surrounding mountain gods, their eyes
peering out of these jungle-encrusted slopes where orchids bud and rise
Nor the chinchillas nesting, nor the shadowy pumas stalking, against
whom the great doors to this place were lashed shut each night.

Here only the sparrows are familiar as they jump from under the bushes.
Sparrows. Pecking at the ground is what they know, scattering is what
they do, before the men hauling buckets of mud-paste grout on their
shoulders down these steep stairway stones today, or before the two
women cleaning the WCs in capri pants and aprons, or before our

Peruvian guide, Irene, with the metal lodged behind her front teeth
who's saying, "Please, leave these windows immediately," to three
teenagers draped on the sills of the openings through which the moon
goddess herself would once glide, where we are shown how the lichen
is quietly eating Machu Picchu, more lichen than ever before, gift
of the bodies of 2,500 tourists admitted and discharged between rising
and setting suns each day.

The wind trembles over this place
clouds billow up from the distant sea
The moon moves through each of her three temple windows
and the sun makes golden passes over stone and spider and
grass as the lichen quietly forms its small circles

To preserve what is here will they someday try to build an exact
replica of Machu Picchu? How will they find another slope for it
in all of Peru? And these particular mountain faces looking down
and these stars so close that Orion seems to be floating on his back
above it tonight, and where will they find the infinite return
of the hearts of the young black llamas and the cries of the maidens
and the ghosts of the little guinea pigs scurrying into their final fires,
and the gliding over all, of the great condor, his white neck fixing you
and me today, arm in arm against the whole of it.

To reproduce all of this, how will they ever find us?

Maximo

The day you refused all food and drink, sank deep
into the mattress, you were dressed in a tuxedo, my love,
and with a joyous look on your face were dancing with a dark
veiled woman.

I called your name, you looked up with languid eyes, "Order an
ambulance," I said in the voice my mother used with my father when his
life was in danger. You looked at me the way he looked at her when
he didn't want to do it, either.

"Just do it," I pleaded, but you were dancing with her and wouldn't stop.
I called the desk, (yes, this is a narrative of sorts,) *Emergencia!* and
fifteen minutes later into the hotel room burst the young doctor and his
aide who always precede any ride to a hospital in Buenos Aires unless you
are *bacán*, a very rich man.

He roused you from your stupor with his strong, still voice. "How do you feel,
Marcelo?" connecting with you man to man, "Like shit!" As he laughed
the gold-edged teeth in his Peruvian mouth glittered, his hand on your belly
pressing a little harder than the other doctors had pressed (including
the TV-series-starlet-MD with ten bangles on her wrist and her lion-y mane).
He whipped through your records. You complained to him about me:
"She's nagging me." "That's normal, man," he returned (sometimes I get
the Argentine Spanish, sometimes not) as he tossed two of your prescriptions
onto the floor…

"*Mira*," he said good-humoredly but sternly. "Get Gatorade. It's the
poor man's IV. Drink water with it, like she tells you. Lots of it."
So now that you're my friend again, I'll tell you the name of the man who
came that day on the white horse with the silver bullets in his gold-framed
Peruvian mouth to save you: Maximo.

And he must have been one good dancer because the dark-veiled lady, she
went with him and left you, tuxedo-less, just drinking Gatorade, watching
TV again, in your pajamas.

The Woman Who Cleaned Up After the Storm

She came after we watched the rain
pour its quantities through the nineteenth
floor, closed windows spilling over the sills
onto the carpets

Shakespeare likened the rain once to the quality
of mercy but that was a gentle rain, this something
else

She came dressed in black carrying a bucket,
an armload of white towels

And as she sopped, wrung out and bucketed
the deluge, her story: how she was the baby seized after the
death of her young parents and raised in a military household
where the General who orphaned her had placed her

The streets of Montevideo move with gusts of warm wind
The gutters overflow into the sidewalks pooling at the doors

How she married a much older man, "A good man," she told us
emphatically, but how do we know that the General of life and death
is not also the General of marriages in this place where the Rio
de la Plata speaks with a thousand mouths?

"Yes, I often wonder who they were, my parents" she said at last
as she moved out of our room with her bucket, her towels twisted in knots
by strong arms, so strong and silent, the woman she has become.

Love on the Cóndor Estrella
November 28, 2016

Old and cranky we argue
barely on time to the bus station
too much luggage
mount the stairs barely
speaking
settle ourselves on the bus top
for the five-hour-long
stare out grass-filled
windows from Mar del Plata
back to Buenos Aires...

This journey the *carretas* once
took fifteen days to make
stopping *at pulperías* along the way for a swig,
now our bus line, *Cóndor Estrella*, moves
its cargo of snoring ones over the new autopista
across the grazing lands of Argentina...

"Look how peaceful the cattle; that's why our meat is
THE BEST IN THE WORLD!" you exclaim.
And we are passing:
Chascomús
Lezama
Castelli
Sanborombón
Maipú
Monasterio as it sits
on the edge of Laguna Chis Chis
(google this word and you will get
"titties" in four different languages)
the grass so silky today, Love,

the light so blue the clouds so melt in our mouths so puffy, so low
the black horse
shining
against the bay horse the white horse lowering its head to drink
cleaning my vision
as we graze on a whole pack of *mani* covered in chocolate
Dolores
General Guido

Coronel Vidal
"Happy?" you ask at the end.
How I love that you asked that
your eyes the color of the lagoon we passed
named for the breasts of my kind!

On the Calle Libertad

At the Petit Colon Bar and Bistro, my window on the Calle Libertad, I gaze into a fiesta of passing *porteño* faces. Just across the square the infamous *Palacio de Justicia* where you were detained and tortured under two replicas of the Ten Commandments which rise in stone off the roof at each corner, and to my right, the tall Secondary School, a small plaque underfoot in the cement:

Aqui Estudiaron:
Marcelo Barroso
Paula Barroso
Fernando Brodsky
Claudio Epelbaum
Eduardo Escabosa
Pablo Alberto Finguerut
Walter Fleury
Guillermo Pages Larraya
Horacio Pérez Weiss
Ricardo Romero
Militantes populares desaparecidos
o assassinados por el terrorismo de estado
Memoria y Justicia

These names and the ones up the street a little further, just across from the hotel where we live and in front of a small Chinese market, these names which always smell of the garbage containers next to them and the urine sprayed over them, pounded by feet and surrounded by a rough mosaic of broken tile and glass...

Mornings we walk past blocks of jewelry windows shuttered tight sprayed with bright monkeys and tigers, elephants and jaguars, a snake, dreamlike face of a jungle dweller in feathered tiara backed by his canvas of leaves, all work of a graffiti collective painted to guard this street of jewelry merchants, each one having had something stolen in his glittering window knowingly, unknowingly, as one competitor here is known to have set the robbers upon his neighbors.

Careful not to catch toes or heels in the uprooted parts of the street, the electricity, gas, water lines, the places where the all-volunteer fire department, the *Bomberos*, can get water...

And just for good measure, in front of one jewelry arcade:

Aqui fueron sequestarios:
Martín Bercovich
Eduardo Ezequiel Merajve Bercovich
Militantes Populares
Detenidos Desaparecidos

Drugged, stripped, thrown from helicopters
into the Rio de la Plata
por el terrorismo de estado
straight from their last walk
on the Calle Libertad.

You Stand at the Edge
April 28, 2016

You stand at the edge of the torrent
white foam spray as lively
as your blown hair, Love,
your arm around her as she leans into your
tall body in her bright red dress

You stand at the edge of Iguazu Falls having delivered
the ashes of your best friend, Carlos, into the waterfall's
diamond spray, Carlos of the deep green-eye-pools and
somberness, yet as you called out to him he danced joyously
for you near his kitchen table in his last days

Her red tongue licks your ear and she whispers, "Come."
She laughs and you melt into a wild nest of butterflies at this
border of Argentina and Brazil, largest waterfall in the world
and it's all I can do to stretch out my veined hand, my rain-
scented wrist to try to restrain you from the long fall…

You stand at the edge and sing the tango of her magnolia
skin, her voice that breaks over you and it's all I can do to
send this poem spinning through air on the brightest wing
to hold you back from her, but perhaps it's asking
too much with you and Carlos at the edge of Iguazu like this,
perhaps it's more than one poem can ever do…

The Poem in All of Its Magnificence
Mar del Plata, Argentina
November, 2016

We are at the top of the top, Love,
and the little people, the waves,
the green sea spouting a pale rainbow spread themselves
at the base of our eyes
surfers surfing for us like black seeds in the
"What's the name of that green fruit we ate for breakfast?"
"Kiwi."
"I'm forgetting the names of everything."
"Me, too."
The rainbow brightens, softens, fills my eyes with tears. The light comes
behind the olden windows still held tight in their crumbly sills up on the
twenty-eighth floor of the Torre de Monatiales as the city of Mar del Plata
moves out into the sea, its red-tiled roofs against white skyscrapers standing
together in the waters. As we sit at our small table in Café de Las Nubes
the rainbow takes off from the sea, flies into the firmament, the poem in its
magnificence carrying us on its winged back beyond where we have ever
been...
You laugh.
"You know what is a *pera*?"
"Of course, a pear."
"When we were young we thought
Juan Perón was a big pera.
And he told us at that time
that Argentina was the only country
where the fishes die of old age.
We ate too much meat."

A name you can't forget.
Where the poem, in all of
its magnificence, lands in Argentina
and begins to weep.

We Summer in the Ancient World

> *"For violence so crushes whomever it touches that it appears at last*
> *external no less to him who dispenses it than to him who endures it. So*
> *the idea was born of a destiny beneath which the aggressors and their*
> *victims are equally innocent, the victors and the vanquished brothers*
> *in the same misfortune. The vanquished is a cause of misfortune to the*
> *victor as much as the victor is to the vanquished."*
> Simone Weil, *"The Illiad, Poem of Might"*

1. The Statues

In Rome the statues all stand priceless in their piazzas and museums even
line the edge of a roof atop the American Embassy where we gaze out of a
window in the Rose Garden Palace Hotel directly opposite. "If we can see
them, they can see us," Marcelo intones, ironic. "Believe it or not, I have
many *anécdotas* of this place during WWII…"

But the statues stand still, is the point, stone corpses risen
or not yet fallen.

The statues are moved only by destiny and the workers hired
to lift them into place.

The statues only kiss as statues
lose arms, legs, heads, phalli,

or, if carved by the great Michelangelo, vulvae too, as he
forms breasts onto the male form, divine.

The statues do not protest.
Napoleon's sister sits half-nude and wed
to Camillo Borghese under the knife of the great Canova.

The statues stare with white eyes as we war and war again,
they, past their time of blood and murder. Bernini sculpts an old man
onto his son's tall shoulder, his little grandson trailing them carrying
the sacred fire of their hearth into exile.

Leaves scuttle across a scorched courtyard where rain once
slid down their faces. The waters of Trevi pound endlessly around them
turning the light blue among the million watching faces.

Is it moth or angel brushing their cheek?
They can never let on.

II. Kiss at Taormina

"We are older than stones," whispers Marcelo
as he brushes my lips.

I've known this for some time, but never heard it
so clearly stated.

Why he's so offhand about all that's human,
Why he's so calm when I rage. We've become
magma standing here in the July heat, the columns of the Greek
Theatre that surround us yet to be. He's done this all before
among the stars and planets. As have I. Why beg for water now?
Why bother to find lunch?
The kiss at Taormina does not speak
of beginnings or of endings.

Our blood stopping in vein
Our hand holding the sword poised over our bent neck
Our tears held in check between one breath
and the next the Arctic ice shelf before it cracks

The blood, the sword, the tears, the breath all waiting:

Our small head strapped into its helmet of hair
before we enter

III. The Stars

And grave to be a star.
To plan it all out.
To twinkle and wait.
Hum our own music into the dark.

A Late Wedding
Yosemite Valley, January, 2017

You said you wanted a garden wedding,
"I've always wanted a garden wedding," you said,
leaving me to wonder about that word "always."
How about this one, Love?
Dusk. The small garden at the rear of the Ahwanee Hotel!
You could stand there all bundled up and watch me
come to you crunching through the snow with hiking sticks
to balance me under a *chuppah* of sky, the massive peaks
ridged with pure white pines holding it up, our ancient parents
long gone.

I just saw the wedding guests coming up from the dark-water creek
in a long row, at least twenty of them, their slender deer legs sinking
into the drifts, nudging each other along, their soft eyes taking me in.
And who did you always want with you in the garden, Love?
And when I come crunching toward you laced with my years
will you recognize me?

I saw they were desperately hungry. On a march of sorts.
We must help them.
They are all we have.

Sing a Song of Scarlet
Trinidad, March, 2018

Here come the bright wings!
Ah! Says the chorus in our long green boat. Ah! Ah! Ah! Ah!
as the flocks of ibis circle in from their feeding grounds
iodine reds coursing through their breasts, their spread of fiery
feathers painting the sky with the song of scarlet.

Swooping onto the green of their island home, and more come, swirling in
from the sunset sea, arrowing over the lake, turning where we rock in
rippling waters, flamingos feeding on the far shore, clouds of trees glistening
with the bounty of flame and song they're collecting.
Did the first people also watch here?
Did the slaves and the slavers, the indentured Hindu, the Spanish, British,
Dutch, heralded by Christopher Columbus in from these seas in their ships?

And did the long boats before them?

The sun dips into the horizon at our backs.
We feel it slowly staining the water.
And still they're flying.
Ah! Ah! Ah! Ah!

What fury?
What ecstasy over steel pans crashing in the sounding waves?
What do they bring to the still trees as they wheel and dive in for one more
night?
And what are they preparing now in their gliding rush
for tomorrow?

Gather the day, Love, press it into your eyelids,
melt it down to its satiny hues
then send it on toward the morrow out of those
brightest of eyes.
For a tall ship sits on the horizon
as our sun sinks down.
What pirate waits to snatch from us a future
we think to be ours? And how long until
our green boat again dances on these waters of delight?
And out of that tall sea-borne vessel
what will come to Trinidad tomorrow?

Paris Without You

Who will ask the cab drivers how much they make and follow their stories
clear back to the Congo, Bangladesh, or Sierra Leone?
Who will tip too little by American standards, hey, that's a whole meal you're
giving away put it in *my* pocket and I'll buy flan and chicken with potatoes
and pasta and carry it all the way home...
Who will say, "Wow!" as the full moon rises exactly next to Notre Dame
while headlights blink into our faces on the darkening Quai and the little old
lady in the print kerchief raises her chubby coated arms to photograph it and
lo and behold (with the boat churning up water and starlight beneath us) she
turns out to be me?
Who will laugh at the babies who yawn as their strollers roll on past Ai
Weiwei's bronzes surrounding the pond like so many demons waiting to
pounce us or exchange sympathetic looks with the pooches under the tables
as their masters tuck in to *steaks au poivre* smothered in *frits*?
Who will order dessert in our old age with so many things we're not s'posed
to eat?
Who will glance at my profile every so often to prove it's still there or long
with me after sleek shoes or say, "Yes, I was just thinking the same thing
myself" as we sit at that cafe at the top of the stairs in Montmartre and watch
the lights turn from yellow to blue?
And who will throw an arm round me as we stumble on and the bum rolls
himself up in a brown checkered quilt over the grate as if it's the Ritz, and
who will pull me back as the gypsy throws a gold ring into the street just
ahead of me, picks it up catching my eye all amazed and tries to trick me
into trying it on?
Who will be the Seine for me?
Who will cheer as my book finds its shelf at Shakespeare and Company to
curl up and snooze upon?
And who will sit with me there at the back of the crowd as some new writer
trots out his sparkling wares before them?

Last Tango in Paris

It's time to say goodbye the way birds do, my love,
whose silent wings pull them apart from each other
through the sunrise-colored air, but our tango remains
moving through the long silver of the mirror at *Le 18*
where we opened a green door and there they were
once more gliding through the illuminated dark,
the tango dancers of Paris! And there we were once more
like the moment we first met, just the little table between us
and click click click the heels of the *milongeros* on the bare floor.
And when we rose to dance, you tall and lean in those cargo pants we once
found on sale on the Champs-Élysées, and on your feet the Argentine
tango shoes that took you all through the streets of the City of Light this
time, and I wearing my mother's dress, she, who left just this spring into
the arms of her own desert night, and on my feet the shoes you once
found for me and the mirror taking us in as mirrors do, *Muchacha, No
Llorés* playing, and I, suddenly weeping there in the midst of those
tango dancers of Paris, and they watching you bend to kiss me
just as the song was saying *"Don't cry, girl, don't cry, people are
watching/Let's dance this tango, the farewell tango/this way
in my arms..."*

It's time to say goodbye the way birds do, my love
who silently fly off from each other through the sunrise
colored air but our tango remains with your soft whisper
"The song says don't cry, my love, people are watching/ let's dance
as before/ embraced really close/ just one soul between two"
and we tangoing on toward the edge of the mirror, and we melting
into the turning dancers, and we with the *bandoneón* swirling us in that
enfolding of dancer and music into its own spinning velvet of time...

How I wish to be there in that room again
little candles burning low on the tables
little roses growing alive in their crystally vases
and you swooping down one more time as the birds do, my love, your
pink eyelids closed, so lovely and tender, as you once more are planting
your little word stars into my teardrop eyes.

Doreen Stock was born in St. Paul, Minnesota, moving to Los Angeles in the fifties. While raising her three children in Mill Valley, CA she wrote two book-length memoirs: *FIVE: The Transcript of a Journey*, detailing family travels through Europe in a VW van, and *My Name is Y*, an anti-nuclear demonstrator's family memoir. She was also a small press (D'Aurora Press) editor and publisher at that time. In February, 2008, she met the Argentine journalist, Marcelo Holot, at the *Confiteria Ideal*, an elegant tango venue in Buenos Aires. On his arrival in San Francisco they began the conversations that led to *Talking With Marcelo, Doreen Stock in Conversation with Marcelo Holot*, a book-length interview (Mine Gallery Editions, in 2017) and the ten-year tango of poems that has become *Tango Man*. For more information visit her website: doreenstock.com.

www.ingramcontent.com/pod-product-compliance
Lightning Source LLC
LaVergne TN
LVHW091321080426
835510LV00007B/598